Horses
For Kids

Amazing Animal Books
for Young Readers

by Annalee Davidson

Mendon Cottage Books

JD-Biz Publishing

Read More Amazing Animal Books

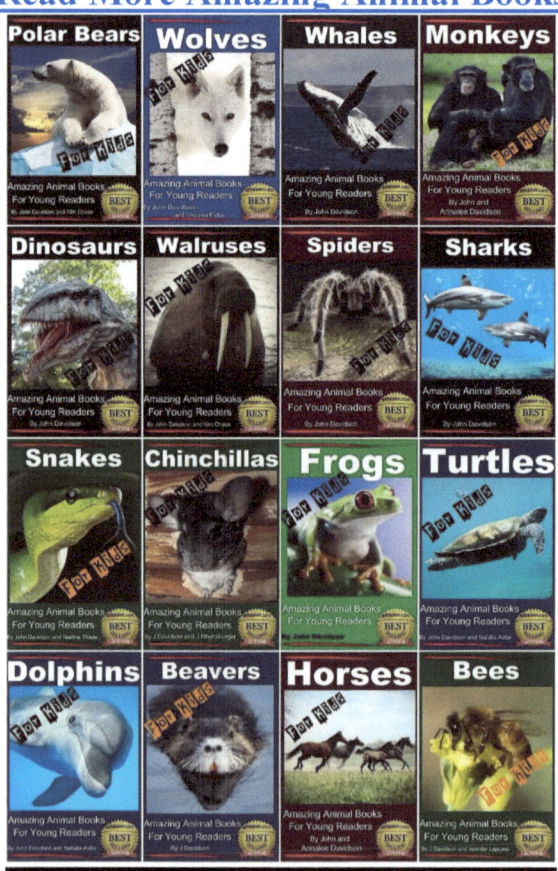

http://AmazingAnimalBooks.com

Download Free Books!
Http://MendonCottageBooks.com

Table of Contents

1. Facts About Horses

Are you already fond of horses at an early age? If you do, you will definitely enjoy the facts that you will learn about the strongest animal we know.

How Horses Are Born

Just before giving birth, a young pregnant horse gets into the right position. During its delivery, you will immediately see the first front foot coming out, followed by the second foot, then its nose. After the head is seen, the shoulders and the head are next, and this is known to be the most difficult part. After this challenging part, the hind legs and hips will come out easily until the baby horse, which is called colt (boy) and filly (girl) is completely out.

Popular Terms for Horses

Horse lovers often use terms which only them can understand. For someone, who is interested about horses, here are some common terms that you need to learn:

1. **Aged** - this is what you call a horse that is more than nine years old already

2. **Backyard horse** - this is a kind of horse that does not live in a barn. Instead, it lives with its owner or master.

3. **Colt** - this refers to a young horse that is less than four years old and has not been castrated yet.

4. **Dam** - this is what you call the mother of the horse

5. **Filly**- this refers to a young female horse that is below four years old

6. **Foal**- this is a baby pony or horse that is still under its mother's care

7. **Mare** - this is what you call a female horse that is already more than four years old

8. **Stallion** - this refers to a male horse that hasn't been

castrated and already more than four years old

How Old Does a Horse or Pony Get?

Unlike people, horses only have short lifespans. Normally, a horse reaches 30 years, but it can still extend up to 40 years old. To determine its age, veterinarians examine and check the incisors (teeth) of the upper and lower jaws.

It is very normal to talk about a horse' speed. The slowest speed is called walk and a bit faster than this is called trot. If you see a little faster than a trot, it is called canter and the fastest speed is called gallop.

2. Breeds of Horses

There are many different breeds of horses and they each have their own unique job. There are some horses that are great at pulling heavy objects while other horses are really good at racing. Some horses are really good as pets that you can ride, but some prefer to be left alone to roam around the field within their herd. Every horse has its own personality, just like every person does, and learning what your horse likes will help you care for your horse even better.

Each of the different breeds of horses has evolved from the same basic horse, which makes each of their unique abilities so interesting. Through changes each time a baby horse is born, horses have developed different looks and abilities. For example, look at the difference between the shapes of hooves from different breeds. Some horses have smaller hooves which help them run really fast, while others have really big hooves which help them stay steady even when pulling the biggest of carts.

There are many differences between the breeds of horses around today, including ears, shoulders, legs, height and weight. Some horses are full grown at only two feet high, such as miniature horses, while others can reach five feet high at their shoulders, which is where horses are measured from. No matter what types of horses you enjoy looking at or owning, each horse will be able to offer something that no other horse can.

Learning about the different breeds of horses can be a lot of fun. If there is a specific breed that you prefer or think is even more beautiful, then take the time to study what makes it different from other breeds. If you are lucky enough to have a horse for a pet, make sure you learn as much as you can about what breed it is so you can help care for it.

3. Thoroughbred Horses

Introduction

The thoroughbred horses are the type of horses that are well known for their use in horse racing. This is because of their ability to run very fast as well as their agility and spirit. They are sometimes referred to as the 'hot blooded' horse.

Origin

The origin of these types of horses is England. The breed was developed at around the 17th-18th century. It was as a result of the crossbreeding between the native mares and the three oriental stallions of Arabian, Barb, and Turkoman breeding which were imported. The breed then spread throughout the world between the 18th and the 19th centuries. They were imported into other countries like the North America, across Europe, Australia, South America and also to Japan. Today there are quite a number of them spread all over the world and approximately 118000 foals are registered every year.

Functions

Aside from their well-known use in racing, they are also bred for other riding purposes such as fox hunting, show jumping, dressage and combined training. Aside from that, they have also been of great influence in the creation of other new improved breeds such as the Quarter horse, the standard bred, the Anglo-Arabian bred among others.

Characteristics

They have a refined head with widely spaced eyes which sit on long, light colored neck.

They have well defined high withers which are evenly curved backwards.

Their shoulders are deep, muscular and sloped whereas the heart girths are deep and relatively narrow.

They have long, clean legs whose tendons are well pronounced and move smoothly in unison

Their upper hind legs are long and highly muscular.

The common colors by which most of them are characterized are, bay, dark bay, chestnut, black, gray roans (rare though). Their faces and legs are characterized by white colors.

© Alexey Stiop - Fotolia.com

Conclusion

Thoroughbreds used in horse racing have resulted in many

accidents and other health problems due to their performance with maximum exertion. The significant American thoroughbreds include; the bulle Rock, the monkey, Janus and Ferrnough, the Diomed the Sir Archie as well as the Messenger.

4. Barrel Horses

© MOKreations - Fotolia.com

What are barrel horses?

These are horses used for barrel racing. This is a game in which the horse and the rider compete with others in completing a certain pattern formed by preset barrels. Barrel racing game is a game majority for women; though at armature levels men can compete. Boys and girls can also engage in the game at youthful stage. The game depends on the skills of the rider in maneuvering the horse in the clover leaf pattern and the horse athletic skills.

The game depends on time for the winner to emerge. The faster the rider and the horse maneuvering in the set barrel patterns, more likely are the chances for them to be declared winners.

Ancient barrel racing

Barrel horses where first used in the state of Texas for racing purposes. A group of women developed (WPRA) in 1948, they all come from Texas. The association consisted of 74 members only. It had only 60 approved tour event at that time.

Modern barrel racing

Timing is carried out using laser system or electric eye as the game is highly depends on time spend in completing the pattern.

While beginning the race for the participants to emerge

winners they have to enter the arena at high speed. When entering the arena the laser system is crossed by the rider and horse hence starts to count. The laser beam keeps on counting till the next crossing during completion of the race. Through these accurate timing are made.

In modern racing the barrel horses used needs to be agile, strong, fast and intelligent to win. The horse has to be intelligent in such a way that it will follow commands of the rider easily and know when to make turns quickly when needed.

Rules in barrel horse race

1. The fastest maneuver wins the game.

2. Running past or off the barrels leads to no time hence no win

3. There is five seconds penalty in case a competitor knocks the barrels off.

4. After time begins there is only 60 seconds to finish the race.

5. Barrels used are always 55 gallon metal barrels which are enclosed on both ends; they must be of at least 2 colors.

5. Race Horses

History of horse races

Racing horses is type of sport, which has a very long history. Records from archaeologists show that horse racing took place in very old Greece, Syria, Babylon, as well as Egypt. Both chariots as well as mounted horse racing were games in the early Greek Olympics by the year 648 BC. Within the Roman Empire, mounted as well as chariot horse racing were the major activities in the industry. Purebred racing was, and still is, well liked by the aristocrats as well as royal family of British society giving it the label "Sport of Kings."

The racing style the distances in addition to the kind of events differ considerably by the country whereby the race is taking place, and several countries have different kinds of horse racings. There exist three main categories of racing namely: flat racing, steeple chasing (which is racing over jumps) in addition to harness racing, whereby horses trot or pace whereas pulling the driver in a bad temper as if it want to throw him or her down. The most important part of horse racing is the economic importance that is in the gambling related with it, whereby in 2008, it produced a worldwide market valued roughly $115 billion.

© NovoPicsDE - Fotolia.com

A variety of horse racing types has given rise to various horse breeds that perform well in particular disciplines of every sport. Breeds, which can be used in flat racing, are as follows: Thoroughbred Arabian, Quarter Horse, Paint, as well as Appaloosa. Steeple chasing breeds consist of the Thoroughbred as well as AQPS. Yoke racing is under control of Standard bred horses in New Zealand, Australia as well as North America, but a number of other breeds, for example the Russian Trotter as well as Finn horse, are found in Europe. Equestrian sports offered entertainment to the crowds as well as polished the excellent horsemanship, which was required in battle.

6. Dressage Horses

In French the word dressage means training. This means grooming and training of horse for taking part in competitions. Through this training the athletic skills of the horses are sharpen so that they can perform well.

Dressage horses make the best use of their riding skills. These are different and can be distinguished from the other horses. They are trained to the physical gestures of their masters and understand their communication. Horses get a very profound effect of training. The riding styles of horses can be divided into two main types mainly the western and English styles.

The western style riding being more famous in The United States of America. The saddle of western style is deeper and larger which is the preferred choice for children. Most children start by learning western riding which will help the children in understanding this sport better. This sport helps in the development of your child. One of the competitive horses riding technique is the dressage. Riders and horses moves together in a chain of technique and movement which is added together to make a workable test.

© Bernard GIRARDIN - Fotolia.com

Dressage horses can be divided into two mainly competitive and non-competitive. The former are a descendant of Europe. These horses are prohibited from wearing bangles, ribbons and other items of decoration. Dressage horses are preferred by the children as these horses teach the rider to be connected. Learning dressage provides more safety than any other style of riding. Dressage horses are the calmest of the other horses which is fun to learn riding on and it gives very little stress.

Dressage horses teach balancing and relaxation not for themselves but also to their riders and it even promotes mental development. But caution should be taken along with selecting the perfect instructor who is caring in nature and teaches horse riding skills with much ease and patience.

7. Shire Horses

Introduction

The Shire horse is one of the breeds of draught horse that is well known for its enormous capacity for pulling weights. Its origin though is not very clear but it is likely to be England. England earns the reputation of first acquiring and producing the Shire breed.

During the late 19th century and early 20th century, the breed was exported in large numbers from Britain into the United States. Its popularity though dropped as mechanization increased (reaching the lowest point between 1950- 1960). It then increased in the 1970s and afterwards although its population numbers are still considered to be low.

Characteristic

It comes in different colors such as black, bay, and gray. The mares and geldings could come in black, bay, gray, or roan.

It has a long, lean head with large eyes which are set on a slightly arched neck. The neck is long and proportional to the body.

© Nicolette Wollentin - Fotolia.com

It has a deep wide shoulder, a wide chest and long wide hind quarters.

Its legs do not have too much feathering. The hairs are fine, straight and silky.

It has been commonly known for its easy temperament.

They are very tall and are the record holders for being the largest and tallest horse breed in overall in various times.

Uses

The Shire horse has a large capacity for weight pulling. It has become popular because of its use in pulling brewery wagons and delivering ales to customers.

It is also used in forestry, leisure and also in promotional pursuits. The smaller ones are preferred for working while the taller ones are used for shows and promotional purposes

Conclusion

The Shire horse breed is very competent in transmitting and impressing its own characteristics to others. It is known for its strength, energy, constitution and endurance. It has been identified though with a risk of a chronic progressive disease which is similar to the chronic lymph edema in humans.

8. Friesian Horses

Introduction

The Friesians (also known as the Frisian horse) are the type of horses whose origin is Friesland in Netherlands. It is the only breed whose ancient origin is Holland. Although they have been refined many times by crossing with other breeds, their strength, endurance as well as their docile nature has been retained. Some of the breeds that they have been crossed with include the Andalusian, and also the desert horses.

Features

They are mainly black in color hence the definite 'wow' factor since the black color is more appealing to many people.

They are always noted for their long, thick luxuriant mane and tail which is often wavy.

© zuzule - Fotolia.com

This makes them a popular sight in the show ring.

Their lower legs have feathers (long silky hairs which are always left untrimmed deliberately).

The pure breed rarely has any white markings.

They have good bone structure with long, arched necks which are well chiseled.

Their ears are short and the heads are that of 'Spanish type'.

Uses

They have been noted for their value as powerful utility animals. In spite of their relatively small stature, they have always been considered as the top war horse in Europe.

They have also been important in the generation of some breeds like the Fell pony and the Dales pony which are native to the UK.

Until today they are still being used on the lands for working and are also popular as carriage and harness horses.

They are also used for riding as well as in the sport of

dressage due to their docile and willing nature.

Conclusion

During the early part of the 20th century, the Friesian horse breed almost became extinct. This was due to their popularity as a trotting horse that resulted in out crossings. Although the out crossing made them faster in speed, their purity was compromised hence there were only three types left at around 1913. This was however rectified at around 1954.

9. Miniature Horses

Have you ever ridden a miniature horse? Miniature horses are very common and very cute. They are mostly found in Europe and the Americas. Some of these horses have black coat, white coat or brown coat; and some of them have a combination of these three colors.

Miniature horses can live for many years; they often live around 25 to 35 years. Their weight range from 150 to 250 pounds; however, you need to make sure to watch for their weight because they can easily get either overweight or underweight. They are considered miniatures horses because their height is around 34 to 38 inches.

Some miniature horses are guide horses. Guide horses work indoors but they stay outdoors when they are not on duty. When they spend time outside they will get stronger and healthier. A miniature horse needs to thrive in pasture, sunshine and a big place to run. During the summer they get think coats; however during the winter their coat gets thick to keep them warm.

If you are 70 pounds or less, you could probably ride a miniature horse. Anyone who weighs more than that should not ride a miniature horse, it can get hurt. If you decide to ride one of them, you have to be careful. Even though they are friendly horses, they can kick and bite.

© Jens Hilberger - Fotolia.com

They eat grain and hay. One square of bale will normally last around three weeks, or just a bit less. So, do you ever wonder how strong they are? Well they can pull three or five times their weight. They might be small but strong.

Do you want to know who the smallest miniature horse was? His name was Bond Tiny Tim. He was 19 inches tall and 30 pounds. He was black and very cute; people could even hold him like a baby.

So if you are 70 pounds or less, ask your parents to find a place where you can ride a miniature horse. I promise, you will have a lot of fun.

10. Mustang Horses

What do you know about the Mustang horse? Here are few facts that you should know about Mustang horse.

© dmitry_saparov - Fotolia.com

1. Mustang horses are free roaming horses found in west America. They are also referred to as feral horse.

2. Their name 'mustang 'was derived from a Spanish word `mustengo' which means stray horses or horses without

owners. Because of these horses reckless nature they are also referred to as wild horses.

3. They live in herds with a dominant stallion ,the stallions breed with their mares where they defend them from being stolen by stallions belonging to other herds.

4. The wild horses are believed to have escaped from the herds of ancient ranchers, Indians tribes, Spanish explorers and settlers who stayed or traveled through America over 11,000 years ago.

5. Native Indians bought the horses at high prizes from Spanish for the purpose of consumption as food and for transportation purposes.

6. In the year 19897 the legislature in Nevada passed laws that allowed the citizens to be shooting any horse that they saw on their sight. This reduced the number of mustangs greatly in Nevada where they used to roam freely.

7. Mustangs received more cruelty in the transcontinental

Railway where travelers where encouraged to shoot the mustangs while traveling to reduce their boredom during their cross country travel.

8. In the year 1924 Pet food industry embarked on horse slaughtering for market where it killed over 500 mustangs per day.

9. About 40,000 mustangs were slaughtered for the purpose of pet food.

10. At the beginning of the century there were almost 2.3 million mustangs on earth, but due to the uncontrolled exploitation they remained only about 25,000 by the start of 1950.

11. In 1959 the first law was put in place to control the cruelty to the mustangs. It banned poisoning and motorized vehicle use in capturing wild horses.

12. Mustangs are highly threatened by extinction due their treatment by people. If not well regulated they may become

extinct soon.

13. Velma B. Johnson was a heroin woman who alongside other wild horse supporters tried to lobby the government for a period of over 18 years to put laws in place to curb the cruelty against the mustang horses. She was later nicknamed by the name Wild Horse Annie.

11. Quarter Horses

For covering short distances that are less than a mile the American quarter horse is the best example. Due to its ability to defeat other horses in races especially quarter mile distances its name was hence founded from that. With their number around three million and two hundred thousand in the world, they are the largest group and they are also well known in the United States.

Over short distances they are known to be the fastest. It is also known well in running competitions, doing work on the farm and in shows. Their strong body is good for some western riding events mostly those that involve live cattle and as a working cow horse. In the western running competitions it is known to make money up to two million dollars in just one race.

Characteristics of a quarter horses

A present American quarter horse has strong back legs and their bodies are usually very muscled hence has a wide chest, short and a small head. For their height, they are usually fourteen to sixteen hands high but the tallest quarter horse is actually up to seventeen hands.

© zuzule - Fotolia.com

Their body types are mainly two: there usually is a racing type and also a stock type. The stock quarter horse type is usually very muscled, short, agile and stocky. The racing quarter horse type is meant to run short distances, hence it is soft muscled and taller. In competitions, the quarter horses are muscled, small headed and also very large in size. Cutting horses are quick, with strong hind legs and very small bodies.

Quarter horses usually are in different and many colors actually almost all. A brownish red color also known as chest nut is the most seen of all. The other colors are black, brown, gray, bay, blue roan and red dun.

12. Breeding Horses

While in today's world most of the horses breed without any human assistance, it can be really useful and beneficial to keep horses as a pet. There is no doubt that horses are adorable and a true friends indeed, so it is meaningful and a good opinion to make them breed manually in order to improve their appearance along with the physical strength.

The male horse is called a sire while the female one is called a dam or mare. Breeding is an easy process as both the parents contribute equally to the offspring.

One can cross breed two species of the horses like "The Arabian Horse" with the native ones to get the desired results. The process of breeding depends on the behavior of the horses and the estrous cycle of the mare. It is the time period when the mare is sexually receptive to the male horse.

The ideal time period for breeding is January, once the sire and mare mate during this period the next and the most important thing is to take immense care of the sire that is the female horse.

During this the sire should be well fed at regular intervals and should be vaccinated for the diseases like EHV-1, the diet should contain a good amount of vitamins along with a huge quantity of proteins in order to enhance lactating ability.

Once the time period of 340 days is achieved the sire is almost ready to give birth to the young one which is called as foal. Proper medical care should be provided to both the mom and the new born baby during this period.

After this the Foal develops and grows up really fast, during the first four months it should be fed with milk and soluble and nutritious food and as it reaches the 4 month mark it would start grazing grass and would start mixing up with the herd.

Hence breeding horses is a great way to get new improved breeds which are stronger, better looking, resistant to diseases and obviously more adorable and loving.

13. Clydesdale Horses

What are the Clydesdale Horses?

Well first of all they are very one of a kind horses. This means that they were made to do a certain job, and over more than 300 years ago, they were used to do farm work in a place known as Clydesdale, Scotland.

This is where their story first began and why they are so very special for being the horses that they are today. The Clydesdale horses of today are the symbol for a very famous beer company called Budweiser Beer, and they have been their mascot so to speak, since 1933.

What makes the Clydesdale horses unique is not just the fact that they are beautiful, majestic, and graceful horses. But also because they are very tall, and have a visible feather, these feathers are all of the very long hairs that cover their lower legs. These long hairs also cover their hooves. Despite the show-off look that these very fine horses do have, they are very powerful horses, and this means that they can pull a load of 1 ton at about five miles per hour.

© Margo Harrison - Fotolia.com

Clydesdale horses are a breed of what is known as being draught or dray horses in the United Kingdom. In America, draught horses or dray horses are called draft horses. These special draft horses were bred to do heavy farm work, and the kinds of heavy farm work, they did included plowing and other types of farm labor.

Though a lot of Clydesdale horses are different as far as breeds go, they are all alike in some ways, and some of these ways is their peaceful temperament, their strength, as well as great patience. Clydesdale horses are indeed a magical type of horse in their own way. Nonetheless, they are also tough, strong, and beautiful at the same time.

14. Morgan Horses

Have you ever heard of Morgan horses?

Origin of the Morgan horses

These are American native breeds of horses. Justin Morgan was the first owner of the horses. It was named after him hence the name Morgan. Justin Morgan was a teacher. He taught in New England in around 1700. The breed possess high strength hence was highly adopted in wars and races.

Characteristic of the horse

Morgan is found in colors such as brown, bay, black and chestnut. Morgan has a wide forehead and short head. The faces may have flat profile or slightly dished. The eyes are large and bright, it has ears that are small and shaped nicely.

They have muscular neck and their heads is always up and straight. Shoulders for Morgan horse are usually deep and angular. They have a broad chest, short and strong back

.They are normally wiling horses when using then in different tasks.

They usually carry their heads higher as compared to other horses. They also have tails which they too tend to raise up more than any other horses in the world.

Keeping of Morgan horses

Morgan horses are easy to keep as they eat lightly as compared to other horses. They can maintain their right body weight while on the least feeds as compared to other horses.

To protect these horses from getting overweight they are sometimes kept on sweet feeds that are reduced in amount.

Uses of Morgan horses

As they are versatile they are mostly used for pulling and driving carriages since historic times.

They are sometimes used in races for various competitions in the world. They are also used in shows such as Pleasure Driving, Western Pleasure and English pleasure.

© Tyler Olson - Fotolia.com

Important facts about Morgan horses

1 .Is the first breed of horse in America

2. Is the official animal for the states of Massachusetts and Vermont.

3. Morgan horses worldwide population is about 125,000.

15. Paint Horses

The paint horses are some of the most beautiful horses. This type of horse is the one that is solid white with large brown spots on it. Most the brown spots are across the paint horses back. This type of horse is most commonly seen in movies where an Indian rides them. Paint horses are beautiful and fun to watch. This type of horse is fun to watch given the fact it commonly has a free spirit. The Indians where known to ride paint horses because they believe they were free at heart.

Horses are some of the most unique creatures here on earth. A horse can help you pull wagons, plow fields, and travel long distances that motor vehicles cannot. So not only are these animals amazing to look at and even own, they are truly one of the most valuable animals here on earth. Cows and other animals are all wonderful, but if you watch old westerns you will see how we even used horses to gather the cows.

© Cécili'art - Fotolia.com

Not all horses can share the same unique style as the paint horses, but all are just as beautiful. Just like dogs or cats the horse has many different breeds and kinds. The breeds can range from simple colors like black or white and its breed be unknown. Like a simple black puppy that you do not know what kind of dog it is. Or the breeds can be like the paint horses, quarter horses, or even a Clydesdale horse. There are so many different kinds of horses and each with their very own history, just like the paint horses. But we will always think of this horse for being the beautiful two colored horse the Indians rode. Paint horses have always been a favorite for actual paintings as well.

16. Riding Horses

Horses are one of the friendliest animals on the planet and are owned by many people as pets. Horses and people have a very long history of working together so they share a very special bond. Before cars, horses where the main source of transportation that people used to get back and forth where ever they needed to travel. Horses would pull a family in a carriage are would wear a saddle and be ridden by one or two people.

Before heavy farming machinery horses were used to plow the fields for many of the fruits and vegetables we eat. Not only were they used to make everyday life easier they were also a source of entertainment.

Horse riding competitions used to be all the rage before TV, radio and video games. People would gather from all around to see whose horse was the fastest and even the prettiest. Today riding horses is still a big sport but lots of people do it just for fun. You can see horses at fairs in the circus and even in some people's backyards. If you have an interest in riding horses and learning more about them, ask a parent to look up a local ranch, farm are horse riding school to go and visit.

© A. Seifert - Fotolia.com

Many farms, ranches and petting zoos allow the public to come in and get educated on horses. You will be able to get an up close and personal experience with a horse by feeding, petting and even riding the horses. Like anything riding horses is something that you have to learn to do before you can be good at it. Working with someone that knows all about horses will help you learn everything you will need to know to become great rider and even how to care for them. Horses are just great animals to get to know and love.

Read More Amazing Animal Books

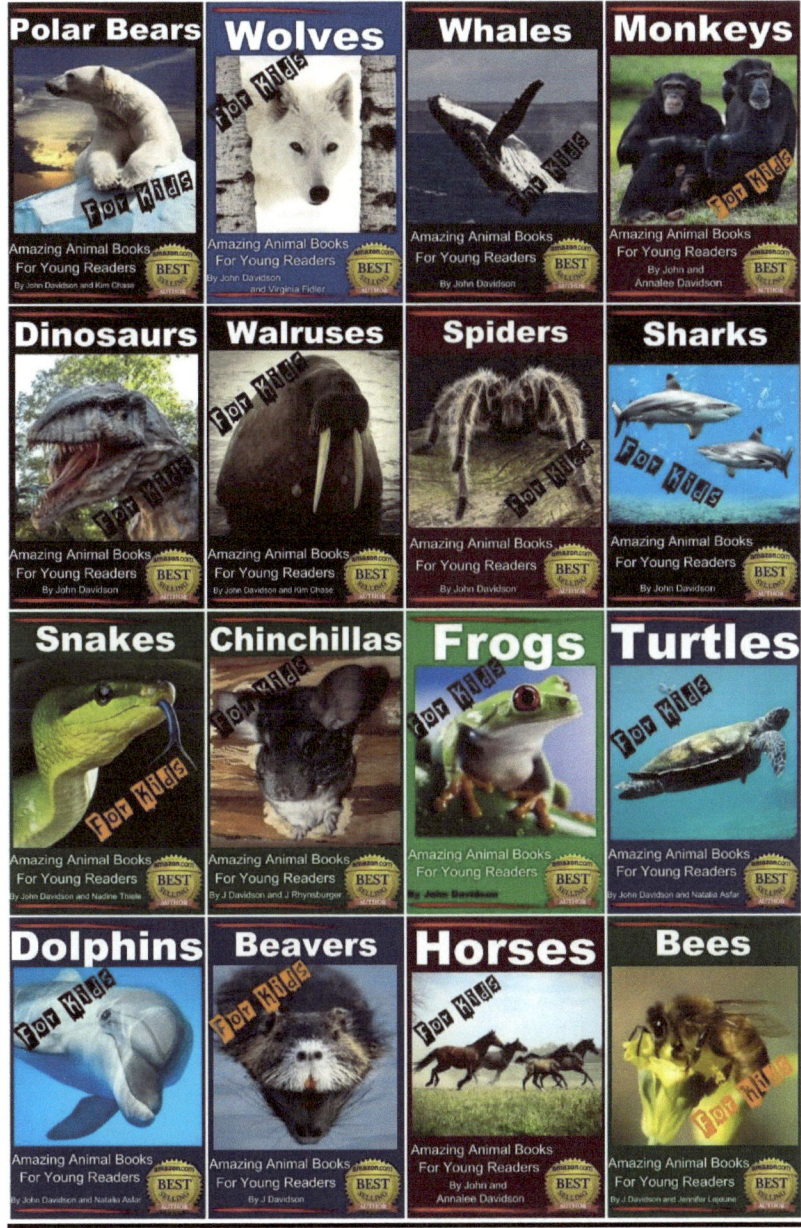

Website http://AmazingAnimalBooks.com

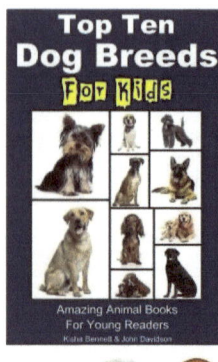

Top Ten Dog Breeds For Kids
Amazing Animal Books For Young Readers

German Shepherds
Dog Books for Kids
K. Bennett

Bulldogs
Dog Books for Kids
K. Bennett

Dachshund
Dog Books for Kids
K. Bennett

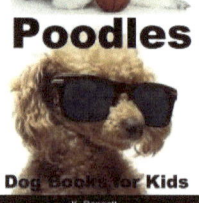

Poodles
Dog Books for Kids
K. Bennett

Labrador Retrievers
Dog Books for Kids
K. Bennett

Rottweilers
Dog Books for Kids
K. Bennett

Boxers
Dog Books for Kids
K. Bennett

Golden Retrievers
Dog Books for Kids
K. Bennett

Puppies
Dog Books For Kids
Amazing Animal Books
By John Davidson

Beagles
Dog Books for Kids
K. Bennett

Yorkshire Terriers
Dog Books for Kids
K. Bennett

Dogs
Top Ten Dog Breeds For Kids
Amazing Animal Books For Young Readers
Zahra Jazeel & John Davidson

Cats For Kids
Amazing Animal Books For Young Readers
K. Bennett & John Davidson

Foxes For Kids
Amazing Animal Books For Young Readers
Zahra Jazeel & John Davidson

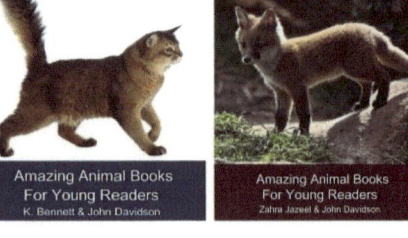

Wolves For Kids
Amazing Animal Books For Young Readers
By John Davidson and Virginia Fidler

Our books are available at

1. Amazon.com
2. Barnes and Noble
3. Itunes
4. Kobo
5. Smashwords
6. Google Play Books

Download Free Books!
http://MendonCottageBooks.com

Publisher

JD-Biz Corp

P O Box 374

Mendon, Utah 84325

http://www.jd-biz.com/

Mendon Cottage Books

P O Box 374, Mendon Utah 84325